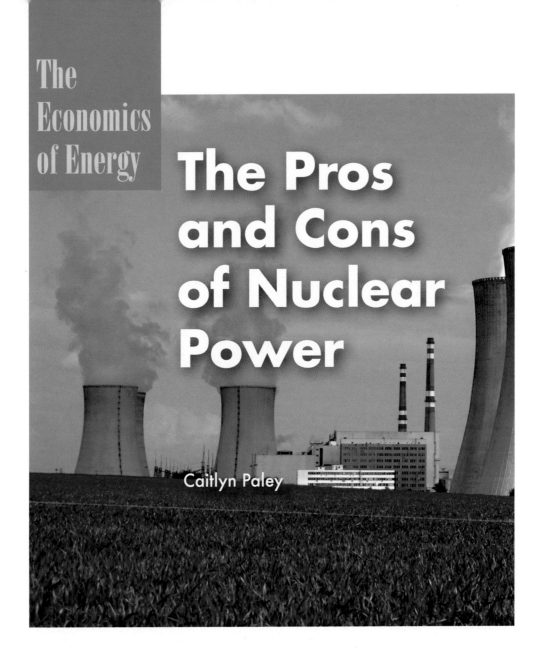

The Economics of Energy

The Pros and Cons of Nuclear Power

Caitlyn Paley

Cavendish Square

New York

Published in 2016 by Cavendish Square Publishing, LLC
243 5th Avenue, Suite 136, New York, NY 10016

Library of Congress Cataloging-in-Publication Data

Paley, Caitlyn, author.
The pros and cons of nuclear power / Caitlyn Paley.
pages cm — (The economics of energy)
Includes bibliographical references and index.
ISBN 978-1-5026-0950-2 (hardcover) — ISBN 978-1-5026-0951-9 (ebook)
1. Nuclear energy—Juvenile literature. 2. Nuclear engineering—Juvenile literature. I. Title. II. Series: Economics of energy.
QC792.5.P35 2016
333.792'4—dc23
2015025672

Editorial Director: David McNamara
Editor: Amy Hayes/Ryan Nagelhout
Copy Editor: Nathan Heidelberger
Art Director: Jeffrey Talbot

Designer: Amy Greenan
Production Manager: Jennifer Ryder-Talbot
Production Editor: Renni Johnson
Photo Researcher: J8 Media

Table of
Contents

Nuclear power plants are located all over the world.
Here a technician in Brazil works to keep his plant safe.

Chapter 1

Nuclear Power through the Ages

Nuclear is an intimidating word. It brings to mind many different kinds of technology. Nuclear weapons destroyed whole cities during times of war. In everyday life, nuclear advances are used in everything from medicine to the smoke detectors in our homes—and then there's nuclear power.

Nuclear power plants around the world convert nuclear energy into the electricity we use in our daily lives. The idea behind nuclear power is actually quite simple. Everything around us in the world is made up of **atoms**. An atom is the smallest unit of matter. Nuclear power harnesses the energy an atom gives off when its nucleus is split into at least two parts. The nucleus is the core of an atom. We use the word "fission" to describe the process of splitting a nucleus.

In the United States, we rely on **nuclear fission** for about one-fifth of our power. Other countries are even more reliant on nuclear energy. France is the most dependent. In France, up to three-quarters of their power is generated by nuclear power plants! The energy we get from these power plants takes the form of electricity. Sometimes nuclear power is also used as a means of heating.

How Does It Work?

In the simplest of terms, nuclear power is the process of **neutrons** colliding. Neutrons are inside of a nucleus. When a nucleus is split, neutrons are released. Fission happens inside of a structure called a **nuclear reactor**. Operators create conditions inside the reactor that encourage each neutron to split one other nucleus. This process is called a **chain reaction**. If more than one nucleus were split by each neutron, too much energy would be given off. The nuclear reactor would explode, which would hurt many people and the environment.

Fission works only with certain elements. Different **isotopes**, or forms of these elements, behave differently in nuclear reactions. We name these differences in isotopes by counting a substance's nucleons (the number of positively charged and uncharged particles in a substance's nucleus). We use uranium in nuclear reactors because it breaks apart during nuclear fission and sets off a chain reaction. The kind of uranium that works best in a nuclear reactor has 235 nucleons. This isotope is U-235. In every chunk of uranium that is mined, only a small percentage is U-235. Most mined uranium is an isotope called U-238. A process called enrichment changes some of the U-238 to U-235.

Okay, but how does a chain reaction generate electricity? There are a few ways, but usually the heat energy created with fission interacts with running water, turning it into steam. The steam spins a turbine attached to a generator. This produces electricity.

The steam is kept in a containment unit. Containment units keep heat in and keep **radiation** from leaking out. Reactors are designed to adapt quickly to changes. Mechanisms make sure that the one-to-one

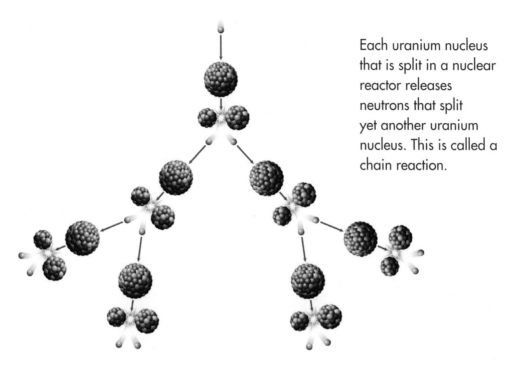

Each uranium nucleus that is split in a nuclear reactor releases neutrons that split yet another uranium nucleus. This is called a chain reaction.

chain reaction stays in balance. Otherwise, reactors automatically shut down to prevent chain reactions from spiraling out of control.

The water that is used in a reactor eventually returns to the lake or river it came from. First, it must be cooled down. Otherwise, the river or lake would get too hot. The plants and animals that live there would die if the water's temperature were to increase. The heated water goes through cooling towers. They release water vapor into the air around the nuclear power plant. The water vapor is not harmful to breathe.

The History of Nuclear Power

Nuclear power has inspired an ongoing debate. Some people think that it is a dangerous power source—one that we should never use. Other people

Cooling towers are responsible for keeping the temperature of water used in nuclear reactors at a safe level.

think that nuclear power's advantages outweigh its disadvantages. People on both sides of the issue make good points. In order to understand these points, we must look back at the history of nuclear power. Nuclear power's history is longer than you might think. Its story crosses continents and traces back centuries to the 1700s.

Martin Klaproth discovered uranium in Germany in 1789. Klaproth was a chemist. He named his discovery after Uranus because another German scientist, William Herschel, had identified the planet in 1781. Little did Klaproth know that his discovery would change the way we power our lives. Mining uranium is needed to produce nuclear power.

Several more discoveries took place before we could harness uranium's power, though. A major step toward nuclear power was Wilhelm Roentgen's discovery of X-rays in 1895. A scientist named Henri Becquerel took Roentgen's work even further.

When Henri Becquerel discovered spontaneous radioactivity in 1896, it wasn't exactly what he was searching for. Becquerel knew about Roentgen's experiments. The discovery of X-rays made him wonder if uranium would emit rays after exposure to the sun. He tested his theory using a photographic plate that worked like undeveloped film in a camera. On the day of his experiment, however, the sun was not out. He put his experiment in a drawer. What he discovered when he opened the drawer changed everything. The uranium had left its image on the photographic plate on its own. Becquerel realized that uranium

emitted rays without any outside influence. He had discovered that some elements are naturally radioactive.

Other scientists, such as Marie Curie, knew about radiation through the work of Henri Becquerel. However, no one understood why some elements were radioactive, and Becquerel

Marie Curie studied radioactive elements in the 1800s. Curie's research led to big discoveries. She even invented the word "radioactivity!"

never used the word *radioactive* to describe his discoveries. One of Marie Curie's biggest achievements was her theory about radioactivity. Curie's experiments, which she conducted with her husband, Pierre, led her to realize that radioactivity comes from an element's atomic structure. Marie Curie named radioactivity in the 1890s. She won two Nobel Prizes for her work, one that she shared with Henri Becquerel.

At the time that Marie Curie was conducting experiments, no one knew that radiation was dangerous. She did years of hands-on work with radiation. Unfortunately, her years of working with radioactive elements like uranium led to her death at the age of sixty-six.

Nuclear Technology and World War II

The biggest leaps in nuclear technology took place during World War II. Nuclear technology actually played a big part in deciding the outcome of the war. The countries involved in the war, including the United States, knew that whoever could develop nuclear weapons first would win. Germany fell behind in this arms race. Historians think that there's a chance German scientists lied to the Nazis and said that a nuclear bomb would need much more uranium than could be mined from the Earth. The United States ultimately succeeded in developing the first nuclear bomb with the help of an Italian scientist named Enrico Fermi. Enrico Fermi was the first person to start a continuous chain reaction.

Enrico Fermi left Italy in 1938. He immigrated to the United States, where he became a professor of physics. He successfully created the first chain reaction on December 2, 1942. His groundbreaking achievement was used in the development of the atomic bomb. Fermi

An atomic bomb destroyed Hiroshima in 1945. This picture was taken from the plane that dropped the bomb, the *Enola Gay*.

was against the bomb, writing with another scientist, "It is clear that such a weapon cannot be justified on any ethical ground … The fact that no limits exist to the destructiveness of this weapon makes its very existence and the knowledge of its construction a danger to humanity as a whole. It is necessarily an evil thing considered in any light."

In spite of his strong feelings, Fermi did help develop atomic bombs. He agreed to help, thinking that the project would not succeed. Ultimately, the United States dropped two bombs on Japanese cities in August 1945. The bombs hit Hiroshima and Nagasaki. Some estimate

A DEEPER DIVE

What Is Radioactivity?
What Is Radiation?

According to the Environmental Protection Agency (EPA), "Radioactivity is the property of some atoms that causes them to spontaneously give off energy as particles or rays." The energy that these unstable, or "radioactive," atoms give off is called radiation. The EPA defines radiation as "energy that travels in the form of waves or high-speed particles." These atoms that give off radiation are easier to split than other atoms. That's why nuclear physicists use these unstable atoms for nuclear fission. Remember that nuclear fission requires a nucleus to split into two or more pieces. Otherwise, the fission would not produce a neutron to continue a chain reaction.

Radiation is dangerous in high doses. High radiation affects people, animals, plants, and even machines. Extreme levels of radiation can kill a person in minutes. Today scientists are very careful to limit their exposure while conducting experiments with radioactive materials.

It is important to note, though, that there are different kinds of radiation. Some forms of radiation are more dangerous than others. The radiation from microwaves and cell phones is called non-ionizing radiation. The radiation from nuclear power plants is called ionizing radiation. Ionizing radiation can be more dangerous than non-ionizing radiation because it can lead to long-term changes in our cells. When a person is exposed to a dangerous amount of ionizing radiation, the body is harmed, and their body attempts to repair this damage. These repairs can actually do more harm than good. A body might make copies of damaged cells, which can lead to cancer. The word "radiation" in this book refers to ionizing radiation.

that the bombs killed 140,000 people, though other estimates are much higher. Some people died right away. Others died later from exposure to radiation. The cities of Hiroshima and Nagasaki were destroyed. Even today, people have mixed feelings about nuclear power because of its violent legacy. It can be difficult to separate nuclear power's role in generating electricity from its role as a weapon.

The First Nuclear Power Plants

After the war, the United States began looking at nuclear technology's potential for good. Scientists knew that nuclear power could do more than just make bombs. Yet it was much more difficult to design the technology that sustains a chain reaction than a bomb that explodes once. This is because chain reactions need to occur in a certain way to stay safe. Detonating a bomb does not require the precision of a nuclear reactor.

When the United States began developing nuclear power plants, the government was in charge of all of them. There were no private companies involved. Laws like the Atomic Energy Act of 1946 said that the federal government owned all nuclear materials. As time passed, the government decided businesses would help create better designs for nuclear reactors. Congress passed new laws making nuclear power friendlier to private business. These laws included **subsidies**, or money paid by the government, to help with the expense of setting up a nuclear power plant.

The government and corporations took a trial-and-error approach to design. Many designs never made it past the drawing board. Nineteen power plant designs were pursued seriously. The government also invested heavily in nuclear infrastructure. These investments added up to over a

A DEEPER DIVE

Women in Science

Several female scientists were key to the development of nuclear fission. Marie Curie's work with radiation in the late nineteenth century laid the groundwork. However, it was Ida Noddock who correctly hypothesized that the isotopes in Enrico Fermi's experiments formed because uranium's nuclei had split. Noddock published her theory in a 1934 paper. Then in 1938, Lise Meitner (working with Otto Frisch) named fission. Each scientist built on the work of those before her. Without these pioneers, scientists wouldn't understand the processes that make fission possible. Female scientists like Curie, Noddock, and Meitner worked hard to overcome the inequalities of their time to produce scientific theories that changed the way we understand our world.

A DEEPER DIVE

The Price-Anderson Act

The Price-Anderson Act has been renewed several times over the years. It will be in effect until 2025. The law has changed over time. The newest version says that every power company is financially responsible if there's a nuclear disaster at any site. Here's how it works: Each power company has $375 million in insurance. If a nuclear disaster causes more than $375 million worth of damage, every power company—not just the one that owns the disaster site—will split the cost of the remaining damage, with each company paying up to $121.255 million per reactor owned. This plan helps spread out the cost of any cleanup efforts following a disaster. The insurance money also helps people who might have to leave their homes. Insurance money covers lost wages, too.

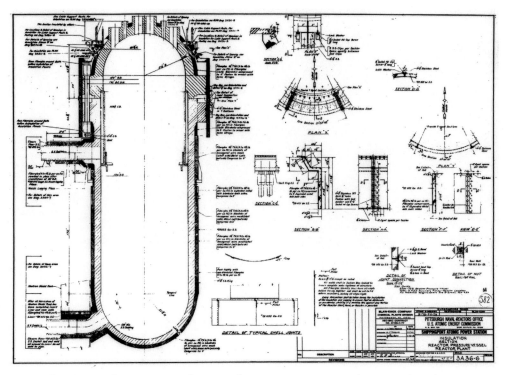

Plans for the nuclear power plant in Shippingport, Pennsylvania. The plant was the first to generate nuclear power in the United States.

billion dollars. That was an astonishing amount of money at the time.

The US government invested that much money so that the United States could have nuclear power as soon as possible. The government wanted to keep up with other countries that were developing nuclear technology. Government officials were especially eager to keep up with the Soviet Union. This was during the Cold War, a time when many countries were racing to have the latest technological advances. Nuclear power played a part in this race.

In order to help encourage innovation, Congress passed the Price-Anderson Act in 1957. Congress wrote the law to protect power

The International Atomic Energy Agency (IAEA) is one of the several groups that regulate the use of nuclear power around the world.

companies if they have nuclear accidents. The law said that power companies were liable, or financially responsible, for only up to $560 million. If a nuclear disaster did more damage than $560 million, then the government itself would cover the difference. That same year, the first commercial nuclear power plant opened in the United States. The plant, located in Shippingport, Pennsylvania, cost more than $72 million to build.

Regulations

The government makes laws about more than insurance, though. It also decides how reactors can be designed. Plans for every new power plant are evaluated for safety. Congress created the Nuclear Regulatory Commission (NRC) in 1974. The NRC is in charge of approving plant plans. The NRC's mission is to evaluate the safety, health, and

A DEEPER DIVE

International Regulatory Agencies

In addition to the NRC, there are international agencies that help to regulate nuclear power. Today, agencies like the International Atomic Energy Agency (IAEA) help nations work together to develop worldwide safety standards. The IAEA also works to connect scientists who can build on one another's ideas. Other international organizations include the International Nuclear Regulators Association and the Nuclear Energy Agency. These organizations work to ensure that nuclear technology is developed according to international standards. They focus on nuclear power's positive uses.

A Timeline of Nuclear Power

1789 Martin Klaproth discovers uranium

1903 Marie Curie, Pierre Curie, and Henri Becquerel receive a Nobel Prize for their ideas about radioactivity

1942 Enrico Fermi successfully creates the first chain reaction

1945 The United States drops two atomic bombs on Japan at the end of World War II

1946 Congress passes the Atomic Energy Act

1953 President Eisenhower delivers his "Atoms for Peace" speech

1957 The United States' first nuclear power plant opens in Pennsylvania

1974 Congress creates the Nuclear Regulatory Commission (NRC)

1979 Three Mile Island nuclear power plant experiences a partial meltdown

1986 A reactor at Chernobyl's nuclear power plant explodes

1989 Stanley Pons and Martin Fleischmann announce they've achieved cold fusion

2011 Three reactors meltdown in Fukushima following an earthquake and tsunami

2012 The NRC approves plans for four new reactors in the United States. This is the first time they approved plans for new reactor construction since 1978

2015 The creation of a new reactor is approved in the United States

environmental issues raised by nuclear technology. Their safety standards change over time as new technology emerges.

Meeting the US government's safety standards can be difficult and expensive. In the past, the government has subsidized the cost of **nuclear waste** disposal sites to help with these expenses. The government has also subsidized the construction of new nuclear power plants and some of a power company's liability insurance.

As time has passed, nuclear power plants have evolved. Power companies were able to overcome the expensive obstacles to implementing the technology with creative design solutions. Today there are about one hundred reactors in the United States, which are owned by about thirty different power companies. Often these power companies welcome visitors to their nuclear power plants for tours. Worldwide, there are more than four hundred reactors in operation. People all around the world use electricity generated by these reactors.

Reactor design has changed over time, and so have the **regulations** governing nuclear technology. People's opinions about the pros and cons of nuclear power have also changed. Nuclear power has had a long history, one that involves many foundational scientific discoveries. Nuclear power's history crosses borders and plays a role in many important events and conflicts. In the end, innovators have been able to harness the power of atoms to produce electricity.

CRITICAL THINKING

- Why might some countries rely more heavily on nuclear energy for power than others?

- Whose scientific discovery do you think was the most important in the development of nuclear power? Why?

- Why did it take so long for scientists to develop nuclear fission?

- What do you think national and international regulatory agencies do day-to-day? Do you think it's enough?

- Do you think that Marie Curie would have conducted her experiments differently if she were alive today?

- What do you think would happen if a nuclear power plant's cooling towers failed?

00-77-1

TOP SECRET
Security Information

Draft #5
November 28, 1953

DRAFT OF PRESIDENTIAL SPEECH
BEFORE THE GENERAL ASSEMBLY
OF THE UNITED NATIONS

When Secretary Hammarskjold's invitation to address this General

Assembly on its closing day reached me in Bermuda, I was just beginning

my conferences with the Prime Ministers and Foreign Ministers of Great

Britain and France on some of the problems that beset our world.

During the remainder of the Bermuda conferences, I had constantly

in mind that ahead of me lay a great honor. That honor is mine tonight

as I stand here, privileged to address the General Assembly of the

United Nations.

At the same time that I appreciate the honor and privilege of

addressing you, I also have a sense of excitement as I look upon this

assembly.

Never before in history has so much hope for so many people been

gathered together in a single organization. Your deliberations and decisions

during these somber years have already realized some of this hope.

TOP SECRET
Security Information

Chapter 2

The Peaceful Atom

In 1953, President Dwight D. Eisenhower gave a speech called "Atoms for Peace." In his speech, he said, "The United States knows that peaceful power from atomic energy is no dream of the future. It is here—now—today." Eisenhower went on to propose that the United States, Great Britain, and the Soviet Union band together to support a new United Nations Atomic Power Authority. He said:

> … to devise methods whereby this fissionable material would be allocated to serve the peaceful pursuits of mankind. Experts would be mobilized to apply atomic energy to the needs of agriculture, medicine and other peaceful activities. A special purpose would be to provide abundant electrical energy in the power-starved areas of the world.
>
> Thus the contributing Powers would be dedicating some of their strength to serve the needs rather than the fears of mankind.

A draft of President Eisenhower's famous "Atoms for Peace" speech—featuring notes and revisions—has been made public and can now be found online.

Nuclear power advocates still believe in Eisenhower's message today. They see an energy source that is reliable, inexpensive, safe, and clean. They point out that there is a lot of misinformation about the technology that gives it a bad name. In short, nuclear power advocates regard it as a misunderstood technology. They fear that these misunderstandings come at the cost of a technology that provides us with electricity.

Nuclear power plants continue to generate electricity, even in bad weather.

Reliability

Nuclear power plants produce electricity in spite of most extreme weather conditions. Consumers know that they can count on nuclear power plants for their electricity. This is not always the case for other energy sources. Coal production, for instance, can be affected by cold weather. Nuclear reactors are designed to operate safely in extreme weather. They are also designed to remain as safe as possible in the event of natural disasters and even acts of terrorism.

The chain reactions that power reactors are engineered to be continuous. As you know, each neutron goes on to split one additional

Radiation is the only by-product of nuclear power plants. Many people call nuclear power "clean energy" because—unlike power plants using fossil fuels—it does not release greenhouse gases.

nucleus in the reactor. As long as there's uranium in the reactor, the chain reaction will continue to produce electricity without interruption.

Alternative energy sources often rely on external factors to produce energy, which makes them less reliable than nuclear power. Wind power and solar power are two examples of alternative energy sources that work best in particular weather.

Clean Energy

Proponents, or supporters, of nuclear power believe that it is a cleaner and cheaper power source than oil, coal, or gas. Research shows that nuclear power does not emit **greenhouse gases** that harm our planet. **Fossil fuels** (oil, natural gas, and coal) release these gases, leading to **climate change**. Climate change is often called global warming. The

A DEEPER DIVE

Abundance

Advocates of the technology say that the abundance of uranium is another reason we can rely on nuclear power. Energy sources like oil and coal require mining and drilling. It takes massive amounts of oil and coal to power our lives. Like oil and coal, nuclear power is a non-renewable resource. It is classified as a non-renewable resource because we will run out of uranium one day. Currently, nuclear power plants need to use uranium as fuel. However, it takes very little uranium to sustain a chain reaction. According to the Nuclear Energy Institute, "One uranium fuel pellet creates as much energy as one ton [0.9 metric tons] of coal or 17,000 cubic feet [481.3 cubic meters] of natural gas."

Nuclear power plants can store large amounts of uranium, and many do. Most nuclear power plants have enough uranium on site to last a few years. Also, it is estimated that there is enough unmined uranium to last hundreds of years.

effects of climate change are severe. As the planet's temperature changes, scientists predict that we will experience drought, flooding, extreme storms, and more. Climate change will impact the way we live our lives.

Many environmental activists see nuclear power as a big part of the solution to the problem of climate change. Nuclear power advocates call the electricity from reactors "**clean energy**" because nuclear power plants do not contribute to global warming. Radiation is the only by-product of nuclear power. On the other hand, coal, oil, and natural gas produce over 30 billion tons (over 27 billion metric tons) of greenhouse gases worldwide every year, according to the US Energy Information Administration.

The Power to Do Good

Nuclear power is viewed as a great solution for developing countries. A developing country is a poor country that does not have access to technology. Often developing countries have an economy based on agriculture. These countries could benefit from nuclear power. Imagine living without light bulbs or the Internet. It's hard to think about how different life would be. Reactors could provide reliable electricity to those who currently live without it. Access to electricity helps speed up the development of a nation.

This is exactly what President Eisenhower meant when he talked about "needs of agriculture, medicine and other peaceful activities." Many proponents of nuclear power say that the technology is a force for good. They argue that the benefits of helping developing nations far outweigh its dangers.

Costs

The cost of electricity from nuclear power is similar to the cost of fossil fuels. While the initial investment needed to build a nuclear power plant is quite high, the other costs associated with nuclear power are actually low. This is true for both consumers and power companies. How do power plants make money after spending so much to build a nuclear plant? Historically, the US government has paid for some of the costs associated with nuclear power by providing subsidies.

The government provides subsidies to new technologies. It's understood that a lot of expensive research has to happen before a technology can make money. That's why the government gives power companies money so they can innovate and still make enough money to pay their employees.

Once a nuclear power plant is operational, the cost of the power is very low. Many activists say that the government will start taxing power sources that hurt our environment more heavily. If that happens, the price of nuclear power will become even more competitive.

Safety

Nuclear disasters leave a big impression on people. They often color their opinions about the overall safety of nuclear reactors. Since nuclear reactors were first developed in the 1950s, there have been three major disasters: Three Mile Island, Chernobyl, and Fukushima. There have been smaller mishaps, including some that have killed plant operators. Yet there are over four hundred reactors in operation worldwide.

A DEEPER DIVE

Climate Change and Conservation

Nuclear power is only one way to fight climate change. Since nuclear power is only a source of electricity, we need to look to other clean technology sources to power transportation. The environmental activists who endorse nuclear power suggest developing technology like electric cars. The other very important part of their message is about conservation. All environmental activists encourage citizens around the world to use fewer resources. They know that a big part of the climate change problem is how much energy we use today. There are simple ways to conserve energy. Some good tips are to switch off the lights when you leave a room, walk instead of asking your parents for a ride when you can, and turn off the water faucet while you brush your teeth.

A DEEPER DIVE

Too Cheap to Measure

In 1954, Atomic Energy Commission chairman Lewis Strauss gave a speech about scientists' hopes for nuclear power. He said, "It is not too much to expect that our children will enjoy in their homes electrical energy too cheap to meter ..." Strauss pointed out many people's hope that nuclear power could be used widely and inexpensively. Strauss's dream hasn't yet come true, but there are many people who believe that it could. These advocates believe that a few changes need to take place first, including new government subsidies so that power companies can build new reactors. They also think that other power sources that pollute the planet should be taxed heavily. If these changes happen, nuclear power will be the cheapest energy source by far.

A photograph from the Ukrainian National Chernobyl Museum shows cleanup crews responding to the nuclear disaster.

The safety record of the nuclear power industry is actually very good. It's also important to keep in mind the circumstances of the three major disasters. In two of the cases, Three Mile Island and Chernobyl, emergency mechanisms were shut off. The disaster at Fukushima happened after an earthquake and a tsunami. The Fukushima circumstances were pretty extraordinary.

Nuclear power advocates point out that the industry's safety record has been unfairly criticized. They compare the safety of nuclear power to other power sources. Coal, for instance, kills about thirteen thousand people per year. This figure does not include mining accidents. That statistic covers only the number of people who die from the effects of pollution. Nuclear power is responsible for cancer deaths and the deaths of those who respond to disasters. Yet some scientists believe that Chernobyl will be responsible for the deaths of up to seventeen thousand people total. These deaths will occur over decades due to

Today's chemical protection suits meet rigorous safety standards, unlike the protective gear worn to clean up the Chernobyl disaster.

cancer from radiation. Nuclear power advocates believe in working towards an even safer industry, but they point out that in the meantime, nuclear power is not the most dangerous power source today.

Many of the deaths caused by the Chernobyl accident were because of improper cleanup procedure. When the cleanup crew worked to stop the spread of radioactive material, they often wore little protective gear. Sometimes the cleanup effort relied on calculations of how long a person could be near radioactive material without getting sick. This is not a best practice for the containment of radioactive material.

New safety standards ensure that responders' risks would be minimized in the event of a disaster. Three Mile Island, in particular, had a big impact on the safety standards for American nuclear power plants. The Nuclear Regulatory Commission developed new safety goals after the accident. They even asked concerned citizens for their input before developing these goals.

The safety of nuclear power plants improves with each innovation in reactor design. Nuclear power plants devote much of their operations

A DEEPER DIVE

Calculating Risk

Calculating the risk of a nuclear power plant is difficult to do. It's impossible to separate out all of the factors that might lead to cancer. Even without any exposure to radiation, a person's cancer risk depends on a number of things. Do they smoke? Is there a family history of cancer? Scientists get good information about cancer risks by looking at big-picture trends. If there is a big spike in the number of cancer cases reported in areas surrounding a nuclear accident, scientists feel confident the nuclear accident is at least partially to blame. These trends are more difficult to observe in areas where people are exposed to low-level radiation.

to reducing risks and refining best practices. Regulations benefit from lessons learned following disasters. In this way, nuclear power plants hope to avoid repeating mistakes of the past.

Long-Term Health Risks

When nuclear technology was first introduced, a lot of misinformation caused panic because no one knew what to expect. Scientists did not spread false information on purpose. However, once the media printed stories about health and environmental risks, it was hard to change people's minds. A big story in the 1960s was that the radiation nuclear power plants release into the air would cause cancer. We know now that the amount of radiation emitted by nuclear power plants is very low. It has been proven that such low levels of radiation will not cause cancer. Yet

some people still believe the original sensationalized story.

Nuclear power plants always look for radiation leaks. Workers monitor the radiation around a nuclear power plant to make sure that the plant is operating correctly. Nuclear power plants are also evaluated by outside inspectors to make sure they are safe.

Geiger counters measure the amount of radiation in a given area. Here someone uses a Geiger counter in Chernobyl.

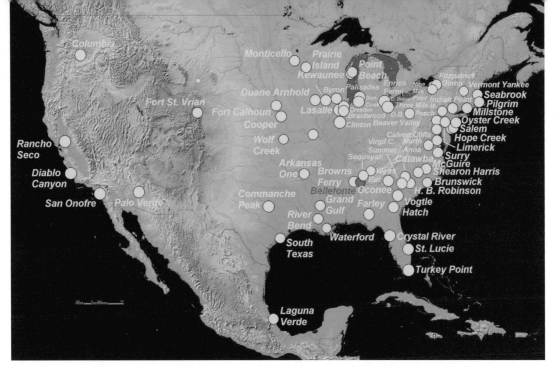

This map shows every nuclear power plant in the United States. Some people say that we need even more plants to meet our energy needs.

The Best Alternative?

Even nuclear power advocates admit that nuclear power has its drawbacks. They realize that there are strong arguments against the technology. It is difficult to deny that there are some dangers involved in the production of nuclear power after a disaster like the one in Fukushima in 2011. However, if the world moves away from nuclear power, we'll need new technology to meet energy demands. Developing new power sources is time-consuming and expensive. It can take up to forty years to invent, design, and implement a new energy source. Many people say we should find ways to improve the power sources we already use. Nuclear power advocates point out that we should employ the technology we already have.

Conclusion

Nuclear power advocates see the technology's use as a positive force in many people's lives. Nuclear power has a number of advantages:

- Consumers can count on the electricity from nuclear power plants because nuclear power is not affected by weather or other factors.
- Nuclear power's fuel source is widely available and will be for hundreds of years.
- Nuclear power plants help emerging nations develop quickly.
- Nuclear power plants have an excellent safety record.
- Nuclear power is a clean energy source.

These reasons combine to make a good argument in favor of nuclear technology. Many environmental activists think that nuclear power is an important tool in the fight against climate change. This is because it is cleaner than fossil fuels. Usually, arguments for nuclear power point out what is wrong with other energy sources. It's important to remember that nuclear power cannot be evaluated alone. We must look at how nuclear power fits into the big picture. This perspective may convince people that nuclear power is the best option we have.

It's also important to remember that many people dislike nuclear power because they do not understand it. It's easy to be afraid of something you can't see, like radiation. Nuclear power advocates feel confident that the more people learn about the technology, the more we'll come to rely on it to power our lives.

CRITICAL THINKING

- Why is it important to have access to reliable electricity?

- Do you think that misunderstandings about nuclear power limit its growth?

- Why does the government provide subsidies to power companies?

- Do you think that nuclear reactors are reliable? Why?

- What do you think nuclear operators can learn from disasters?

- Do you think nuclear energy is a good solution to climate change? Why?

An atomic bomb called "Fat Man" razed the Japanese city of Nagasaki, killing tens of thousands of people.

Chapter 3

The Disadvantages of Nuclear Power

Nuclear power isn't just used for good. Beyond providing us with electricity, nuclear advances have been used to manufacture weapons unlike anything available in the nineteenth century. Experts have described the contrast between nuclear technology's uses as the "Dr. Jekyll/Mr. Hyde character of the atom."

Dr. Jekyll and Mr. Hyde are the main characters of a novella by Robert Louis Stevenson. Dr. Jekyll is a scientist who develops a concoction that transforms him into Mr. Hyde. Dr. Jekyll was looking for a way to eliminate all of the bad parts of his personality. Unfortunately, his plan didn't work. Instead he became Mr. Hyde, a murderer with no sense of right and wrong.

The Dr. Jekyll/Mr. Hyde comparison captures the fact that nuclear technology can be used to power our homes and advance society, like the successful scientist, Dr. Jekyll. But it can also be used to kill, like Mr. Hyde.

People are aware of nuclear technology's role in World War II. Nuclear power often brings to mind the bombing of Hiroshima and Nagasaki. The dark history of nuclear power colors the opinions of many. Some feel it is impossible to look beyond the destruction nuclear technology has brought to the world.

By some estimates, the nuclear bombs dropped on Japan killed 140,000 people. Since World War II, peacekeepers have pointed out that nuclear power plants are a big risk in unstable countries. The fear is that nuclear power plants in war-torn regions could actually be nuclear weapons plants in disguise.

Some people also fear that nuclear power plants don't do enough to secure their facilities. Security is crucial. The threat of terrorism has been a pressing concern in the United States since the terrorist attacks on September 11, 2001. Counterterrorism experts recognized the threat nuclear power plants could pose even back in the 1950s. If terrorists were able to enter a nuclear power plant and intentionally release radiation, thousands of lives could be lost. Sometimes the fuel used in reactors causes concern, too. Uranium cannot be used to make a nuclear weapon, but plutonium can. There are nuclear power plants around the world that use plutonium as fuel. American nuclear power plants, however, do not use plutonium because of the risk of terrorism.

Nuclear Disasters

So far, terrorists have not targeted nuclear power plants. But intentional disasters are not the only concern. Accidents at nuclear power plants have happened.

Nuclear fission can be a risky process, and the stakes are higher than mining coal or drilling for oil. When something goes wrong at a nuclear power plant, the impact on people, animals, and the environment can be devastating. Nuclear physicists and engineers think a lot about preventing disasters when designing nuclear power plants. They try to imagine every scenario and build in solutions to avoid disasters. There are two types of nuclear disasters: reactor meltdowns and nuclear explosions. Both types spread harmful levels of radiation over large areas. Sadly, both kinds of disasters have occurred.

Three Mile Island

On March 28, 1979, the Three Mile Island nuclear power plant in Pennsylvania had been in operation for three months when something went terribly wrong. On that day in March, a small equipment failure set in motion a chain of events with big consequences.

After the equipment failed, operators made some mistakes that made a bad situation even worse. Instead of adding more water to an overheated reactor, they drained the water further. Draining the water raised the temperature of the reactor until a partial meltdown occurred.

Meltdowns occur when a nuclear reactor overheats. It's a very literal term. During a meltdown, the overheated rods eventually melt the reactor. If the uranium fuel rods in a reactor get too hot, they can emit levels of radiation that destroy the surrounding environment. High levels of radiation cause lasting health effects in people and animals.

Nuclear power plants are always located near water because water is an important part of transforming uranium into electricity. A steady

A sign marks the site of the Three Mile Island nuclear disaster in Pennsylvania.

flow of water keeps the reactor at a constant temperature. Unfortunately, this nearness to water can be devastating if a disaster occurs. If radiation seeps into the water after a complete meltdown, it spreads far and wide.

Luckily, the radiation at Three Mile Island did not reach any water sources. The partial meltdown was still very dangerous, however. People living in the surrounding area had to evacuate until it was safe to return. The cleanup process was expensive. Many people began to doubt the safety of nuclear power as they watched the disaster on the news.

Chernobyl

Seven years later, the world witnessed the horrible consequences of a nuclear explosion. Nuclear explosions spread much higher levels of radiation much farther from the disaster site. The Chernobyl disaster took place on April 26, 1986. Operators were running a test on their plant,

One of Chernobyl's reactors was destroyed by a nuclear explosion in 1986.

which is located in Ukraine—then part of the Soviet Union—near the border with Belarus.

To complete their test, they disabled their reactor's emergency core-cooling system. This system was designed to prevent meltdowns and explosions. Emergency mechanisms should never be disabled. Like the disaster at Three Mile Island, this was not the only thing that went wrong. Operators set the power of the reactor much too low. This caused some equipment to fail. Despite the operators' best efforts to avoid disaster, the reactor exploded. The explosion immediately started spreading radiation. Two workers died on the day of the explosion.

Unfortunately, they were the first of many to die. Twenty-nine more people died in the following months due to radiation exposure. One estimate says that cancer linked to the explosion will kill nearly twenty thousand people between 1990 and 2040. Chernobyl is proof that nuclear accidents have a wide-ranging and long-lasting impact.

The radiation in the area closest to the reactor reached fatal levels. Over three hundred thousand people were evacuated from their homes.

A DEEPER DIVE

What Is Acute Radiation Syndrome (ARS)?

Acute Radiation Syndrome is caused by exposure to dangerously high doses of radiation. ARS hurts a person's immune system. Symptoms of ARS include nausea, vomiting, and burned skin. An ARS patient might get sick right after exposure. Sometimes it takes time for symptoms to appear. Many ARS patients need blood transfusions and bone marrow transplants to help heal their immune systems. Extreme cases of ARS result in death, but most ARS patients get better with time. However, there can be long-term effects of radiation exposure. ARS patients face an increased risk of cancer.

The exclusion zone, the name for the evacuated area surrounding Chernobyl, remains abandoned decades later.

Imagine leaving your house today and never going back. That's what happened to the people living around Chernobyl. They lost their belongings. They lost their communities. Many people, like farmers, lost their ability to make a living. They worried about their health and the health of their families. They all had to start over somewhere new. Sometimes the people in their new communities were afraid of being around them. Chernobyl changed the whole course of these people's lives.

Radiation spread all over Europe. The evacuated areas around Chernobyl have never been reopened. The affected area is still behind a gate. Scientists and government officials are allowed to enter—but only for a short time. This restricted area is called the exclusion zone.

Decontamination

After the explosion, officials struggled to prevent more explosions from happening. The reactor caught fire after the first explosion. Putting it out was difficult. It was also dangerous. The first two people to die at Chernobyl were firefighters. They weren't wearing protective gear because they didn't know they were being exposed to radiation. The fire kept raising the temperature of the reactor, which likely did even more damage. Firefighters, miners, members of the military, and others managed to put out the fire. They prevented an even bigger tragedy.

Then the cleanup began. In the end, the cleanup in and around Chernobyl cost up to four times the money the whole country's nuclear program made. A team of six hundred thousand people called the **liquidators** went from house to house. They made sure that everyone had evacuated, and they started demolishing houses and disposing of radioactive debris. The liquidators were exposed to different amounts of radiation. Their exposure depended on how close they were to the blast site and how soon after the explosion they started their work.

Today, the liquidators face many health problems. They have higher than normal rates of cancer, cataracts, and cardiovascular disease. Some liquidators have also passed health issues down to their children. Radiation has affected many liquidators' genes. Genetic mutations may be passed on for generations.

The nuclear disaster at the Fukushima Daiichi power plant was caused by an earthquake and the resulting tsunami.

Fukushima

Not all disasters are caused by equipment failures and human errors. Critics of nuclear power say that there are also circumstances beyond our control. They point to the disaster at Fukushima as evidence.

In 2011, an earthquake in the Pacific Ocean followed by a tsunami caused meltdowns in not one but three reactors at the Fukushima Daiichi power plant in Japan. Emergency workers responded quickly. They followed best practices for cleanup. About 160,000 people were

A DEEPER DIVE

Radioactive Milk?

In order to decide on safe levels of radiation, scientists conduct experiments. Generally, scientists use mice to complete these experiments. They expose mice to different levels of radiation and observe the effects. Then they make safety recommendations. The US government keeps these recommendations in mind after a nuclear disaster. We do not import food from affected areas until it is safe to do so. It can take a long time for milk and meat to meet safety guidelines after a nuclear disaster. Animals like cows keep eating grass that is contaminated, which causes their milk to be radioactive.

evacuated as soon as possible. As a result, there were no deaths and two-thirds of responders face no increased risk for cancer. Sadly, the citizens who lived closest to the reactors and the other one-third of responders face a significant risk of developing cancer.

The natural circumstances that led to the disaster were unavoidable. Anti–nuclear power activists argue that what happened in Japan could happen elsewhere. They say that there are too many factors to consider nuclear power safe.

Everyday Environmental Impacts

Environmental activists don't just worry about the negative consequences of nuclear power after a nuclear disaster. There are environmental considerations in the day-to-day operations of a nuclear power plant.

Nuclear Waste

Before it is used in a nuclear power plant, uranium is made into a fuel rod. Fuel rods are what go inside of nuclear reactors. Each fuel rod can only be used for a certain amount of time before it is used up. A rod usually lasts for a maximum of two years. We call used up rods **"spent rods."** Spent rods must be disposed of carefully. They contain extremely high levels of radiation. Radiation decreases naturally over time. However, the radiation in spent fuel rods takes tens of thousands of years to disappear! Most spent rods are stored on site at a nuclear power plant. This storage is just a temporary solution, though.

The spent fuel rods are very hot. They must be kept cool in order to prevent radiation from leaking out. Most nuclear power plants keep spent

Spent rods must be stored in a permanent storage facility to prevent the contamination of our water.

fuel rods under running water to keep them cool. Unfortunately, each power plant only has so much space to store spent rods.

Permanent storage of spent fuel rods is a tricky balancing act. First, spent fuel rods must be transported to a permanent storage site. Toxic nuclear waste is driven from a nuclear power plant to a packaging facility. The packaging facility makes sure the spent rods won't leak. Next the spent rods travel again, this time to the permanent storage site. Anti–nuclear power activists point out the danger of transporting nuclear waste. What happens if there is a car accident? What if terrorists steal the toxic material? And where should spent fuel rods end up?

High-level nuclear waste is only one kind of nuclear waste. Low-level nuclear waste is what we call any equipment or safety gear that comes into contact with radiation. Low-level waste needs to be disposed of, too. Low-level waste goes to nuclear waste dumping sites in each state. Many people living around these dumping sites don't like the idea that nuclear waste is so close to their homes. They worry about possible effects on their health.

Conclusion

Nuclear fission is pretty simple, but making sure nuclear power plants stay safe is not. Nuclear reactors' safety mechanisms can fail for a number of reasons. These failures can affect the chain reactions happening inside of reactors. Sometimes failures cause chain reactions to produce more than one neutron per atom. If those extra neutrons go on to split other atoms, they create too much heat energy. This extra heat can cause a nuclear disaster.

Nuclear disasters take the form of meltdowns or explosions. Disasters release dangerous levels of radiation. People, animals, and the environment are affected by that radiation. High levels of radiation destroy our cells, and exposure to high levels of radiation causes cancer, radiation sickness, and other health problems. It also causes long-term effects like birth defects. Nuclear disasters even make crops unsafe to eat. Sometimes the land around a disaster is never safe to live on again. Finally, these disasters cost billions of dollars to clean up.

Nuclear disasters are the main reason that people protest nuclear energy, but there are other reasons, too. The uranium and plutonium

A DEEPER DIVE

Yucca Mountain

Currently, there is no long-term storage solution for nuclear waste. There is one site designed for high-level nuclear waste called Yucca Mountain. Spent fuel rods are considered high-level nuclear waste. High-level nuclear waste is dangerous and must be handled carefully. The government and private companies have spent $15 billion developing Yucca Mountain. The facility has never opened because many citizens living nearby worry about their exposure to radiation.

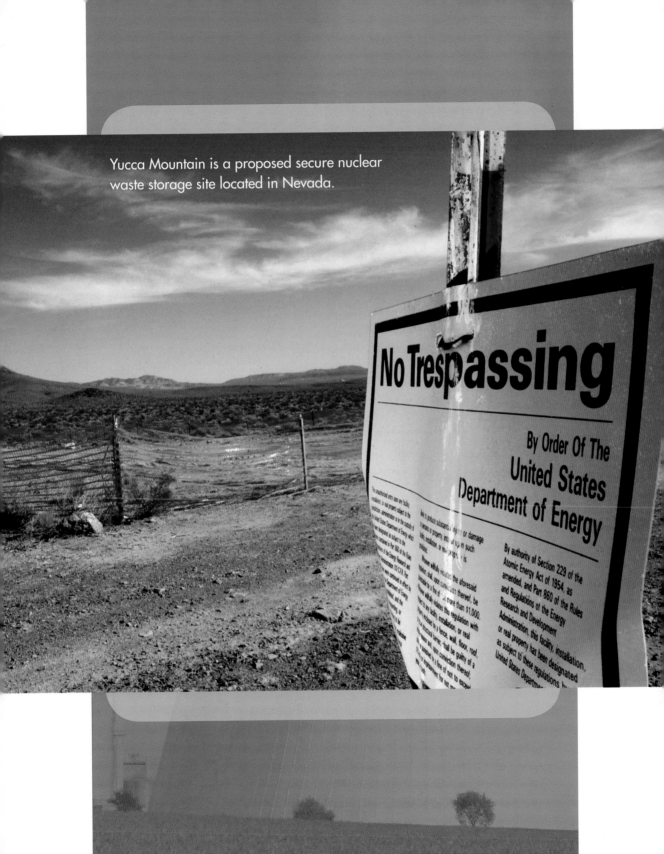

Yucca Mountain is a proposed secure nuclear waste storage site located in Nevada.

Activists come together to protest the Indian Point nuclear power plant in New York.

used in nuclear reactors could be used by terrorists to do a lot of damage. The governments of unstable countries might use uranium and plutonium to make nuclear weapons.

Nuclear power affects the environment even when everything goes right. Mining uranium ruins the land and releases greenhouse gases. Nuclear waste stays radioactive for thousands of years and must be stored somewhere.

Aside from the dangers of nuclear power, it is expensive to build nuclear power plants. Both the government and private companies have spent billions of dollars developing nuclear power technology. Critics think that these reasons make nuclear power a bad solution to our energy crisis.

CRITICAL THINKING

- What would be the hardest part of leaving your home forever?

- Do you think other kinds of fuel are safer than nuclear power?

- Would you want nuclear waste stored near your home?

- How are nuclear disasters different from natural disasters like hurricanes?

- Do you think that critics make good points about nuclear power? Which criticisms do you agree with?

- Do you think that Yucca Mountain is a good solution for long-term storage of nuclear waste? Why?

- How would you store radioactive waste?

Tokamak reactors are an example of a new technology that could make nuclear power more widely available.

Chapter 4

Looking Forward

Nuclear power is a hotly debated technology, but as of now it is a significant source of our electricity. In fact, the next decade could bring an expansion of nuclear power. Power companies in the United States are applying to build new nuclear power plants in record numbers. The Nuclear Regulatory Commission has approved plans for five new reactors since 2012.

While the proposed reactors are based on existing designs, engineers continue to improve nuclear fission. Some innovators are looking beyond current nuclear technology. There are those who believe fission is not the best way to harness uranium's power. Others are developing systems that do not require uranium at all.

Nuclear fusion, breeder reactors, and small modular reactors could change the way nuclear power is generated. They could also help ensure everyone has access to affordable electricity. Other innovations aim at solving problems of nuclear waste storage. Like nuclear power itself, these innovations have pros and cons.

Nuclear Fusion

Nuclear fission is the process of separating the nucleus of an atom. Nuclear fusion is the opposite process. Nuclear fusion is when two nuclei combine. Nuclear fusion is a natural process. The energy that the sun gives off comes from nuclear fusion.

There are many obstacles to man-made nuclear fusion. Nuclei repel each other. Think about what happens if you try to put the positive sides of two magnets together. This is exactly how nuclei behave—they push each other away.

The other big obstacle to fusion is that it requires a very high temperature, a temperature over 180 million degrees Fahrenheit (100 million degrees Celsius). Making fusion happen takes a lot of power. Scientists have achieved fusion, but right now it takes more power to heat a reactor than we get out of it.

Countries around the world are researching ways to make fusion practical. No one has made enough progress for fusion to power our electricity. There are exciting developments, though. New research and development in tokamak reactors are seeing promising results as fusion reactors. Several countries are experimenting with them today and seeing promising results. France in particular is testing a state-of-the-art tokamak reactor.

Fusion is desirable because it emits helium, which is completely safe. Fusion requires two special kinds of hydrogen atoms called deuterium and tritium. These are superior to uranium in a few ways. Deuterium comes from the ocean. There will never be a shortage of deuterium. On the other hand, tritium is man-made. It's also radioactive. The benefits of

A DEEPER DIVE

The Future of Uranium

Nuclear power is not a renewable resource. This is because nuclear fission requires uranium. There is only so much uranium that can be mined. Yet uranium stretches farther than other non-renewable resources. It takes less to make more energy. Only a small amount of uranium is needed for nuclear fission. There is also a lot of uranium left on Earth. Power companies often have enough uranium on site to last for years. Some people worry about what will happen when we run out of uranium. This fear is one reason that scientists are looking at developing nuclear fusion. Nuclear fusion uses resources that are more abundant.

Most nuclear power plants rely on uranium, which must be mined from deep in the ground. Innovators are looking for ways to run nuclear power plants without uranium before the fuel source runs out.

tritium are that it's inexpensive and it loses its radioactivity much, much faster than spent fuel rods of uranium. The rapid loss of radioactivity also makes it easier to store.

What are the benefits of nuclear fusion?
- Fusion uses tritium and deuterium instead of uranium.
- Tritium is less radioactive than uranium.

What are the drawbacks?
- Fusion is difficult to achieve.
- So far no one has produced much energy from fusion.

Fast Breeder Reactors

Fast breeder reactors work the same way as the reactors currently in use in our nuclear power plants. Fast breeders use nuclear fission to produce electricity. The key difference is the fuel that fast breeder reactors use. Fast breeder reactors use uranium to create plutonium that results from fission. This plutonium is **reprocessed** so that it can be used again. Fast breeder reactors create more fuel than they started with. Fast breeder reactors are thus said to produce, or "breed," their own fuel.

Another difference between fast breeder reactors and more commonly used reactors is the kind of moderators they use. Moderators help control the speed of neutrons inside of the reactor. The kinds of reactors used in the United States right now require that neutrons be slowed down to sustain a chain reaction. Fast breeder reactors use a moderator that allows neutrons to move very fast.

The United States does not currently use fast breeder reactors. There are two reasons that breeder reactors are considered dangerous. First, reprocessed plutonium is used in certain nuclear weapons. Stores of reprocessed plutonium could be targets for terrorists. Reprocessing plants work with highly radioactive materials, too. These factors make fast breeder reactors a risky choice

Operators cannot come into contact with plutonium while they work. Instead they must "handle" the plutonium from behind eight layers of glass!

Cold Fusion:
A Failed Experiment

In 1989, two scientists said they'd overcome the obstacles of fusion. They called their process cold fusion. Stanley Pons and Martin Fleischmann said their process did not need any fancy equipment. Pons and Fleischmann believed they had developed an idea that could change how the world gets electricity. The two scientists shared some of the details of their process with Steven Jones, another scientist who wanted to work with them. The three did not end up collaborating, but Jones wanted to publish a paper together anyway. Pons and Fleischmann became afraid that they wouldn't get credit for their idea. They quickly put together a paper and held a press conference.

The scientific community was very excited about this innovation—that is until no one else could make it work. Cold fusion was not what it seemed. Other scientists realized that Pons and Fleischmann made big assumptions in their experiments. Still, cold fusion inspired many

people to think about innovations in nuclear power. There are still scientists who think cold fusion is possible. These scientists continue to experiment with cold fusion.

in lawmakers' eyes. In 1977, President Carter banned nuclear power plants from reprocessing plutonium.

Other countries do currently use fast breeder reactors, though. There are four countries today that have fast breeder reactors in operation: Russia, India, China, and Japan. It's possible that the United States could employ breeder reactors one day. There are also other kinds of breeder reactors in development.

What are the benefits of fast breeder reactors?
- Fast breeders reactors use less uranium.
- Fast breeder reactors produce more fuel than they started with.

What are the drawbacks?
- Breeder reactors are a developing technology.
- Fast breeder reactors require plutonium, which could be used in acts of terrorism.
- Plutonium is very radioactive.

Small Modular Reactors

An emerging nuclear technology is the small modular reactor (SMR). This reactor's name is a good description of what it is. These reactors are much smaller in size than a typical nuclear reactor. They are also built using pre-made pieces, or modular, in construction. There are many benefits to having a small modular reactor.

First, SMRs are less expensive to build than a full-sized reactor. The lower cost is because they are smaller. It is easier to move the pre-made pieces, too. Because SMRs are so portable, they open up the opportunity for less developed countries to have access to nuclear power. Trucks can move pre-made pieces of SMRs. A country wouldn't need to have a lot of extra technology to construct a nuclear power plant.

Another advantage of SMRs is that they use less fuel because of their size. Small modular reactors are safer because they contain less radioactive material. In the event of a nuclear disaster, less radiation could be spread. They also use less water, which is better for the health of water sources. These factors are all good news for the four billion people who have little to no electricity in developing countries. Developing countries often rely on neighboring nations for some of their energy needs. Other developing countries simply make do without newer technology, like nuclear reactors. This might prevent them from meeting their citizens' energy needs.

What are the benefits of small modular reactors?
- SMRs are safer than larger fission reactors.
- They can easily meet the power needs of a developing country.
- SMRs are easier to build (sometimes they are even pre-made).
- SMRs require less water.

What are the drawbacks?
- SMRs do not produce as much electricity because they are smaller.
- SMRs still have the risks associated with larger fission reactors.

The Future of Nuclear Waste Containment

Innovations aren't just limited to new kinds of reactors. Some innovations address other issues related to nuclear power, like what to do with nuclear waste. Right now, nuclear power plants are still storing high-level waste on site as a short-term solution. The United States is still developing long-term solutions for nuclear waste. The most developed plan is the nuclear waste containment site called Yucca Mountain. Yucca Mountain is in Nevada's desert. The ground at Yucca Mountain is volcanic rock, and the site is not near any water. Water is an important consideration for any proposed nuclear waste site because water can spread radiation.

The government and private companies have been working on the Yucca Mountain site since the 1970s. The site has cost over $15 billion so far. Political opposition to the site has prevented it from opening yet. Most

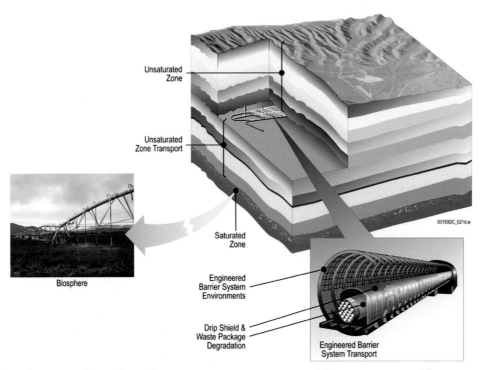

This diagram shows how the Yucca Mountain site would use engineered barriers as well as volcanic rock to secure nuclear waste.

A DEEPER DIVE

Energy Independence

Small modular reactors bring up a larger issue—energy independence. A country achieves energy independence when it does not rely on other countries for fuel or power.

Bulgaria is a great example of a developing country that is aiming for energy independence. Bulgaria is currently tied to a neighbor for its energy needs. All of Bulgaria's nuclear power comes from Russia. This reliance comes at a cost. Russia gets a say in Bulgaria's decisions because Bulgaria depends on Russia for its nuclear power and most of its gas. Nuclear power advocates say that advances in nuclear reactors, like SMRs, could make a big difference for countries like Bulgaria that aren't energy independent.

Energy independence is a major issue of our day. Relying on other countries for resources like oil often causes tension. Innovators in the United States look for ways to power the country without resources from other nations. New technology could make that goal a reality.

recently, Yucca Mountain was part of Barack Obama's campaign promise to the citizens of Nevada. While campaigning, President Obama said that he would make sure that the site didn't open if he became president. The people of Nevada are nervous about the dangers of nuclear waste and don't want it stored near their homes. Despite this opposition, it looks like Yucca Mountain might open soon. Nuclear power plants are running out of space to store nuclear waste. On-site storage was never meant to be a long-term plan.

When Yucca Mountain (or any other containment site) opens, high-level nuclear waste will be transported across states. Trucks will carry this waste on our highways. Some people wonder how safe this will be. So far, there's never been a severe accident during the transport of low-level nuclear waste.

Yucca Mountain is an innovative solution to waste storage. The Nuclear Regulatory Commission has evaluated the site and believes that no radiation or radioactive material could escape from storage there. Scientists studied what would happen if there were a natural disaster, what would happen to the radioactive material over time, and whether or not people could easily trespass at the facility.

An Uncertain Future

It's difficult to tell if nuclear power is a technology that is here to stay. Some countries, like Germany, have begun shutting down their nuclear power plants. Germany decided to move away from nuclear power after the Fukushima disaster. In the United States, there is a lot of opposition to nuclear power.

Citizens all over the world come together to protest nuclear power. They make it clear they don't want nuclear power plants or nuclear waste sites in their communities.

A DEEPER DIVE

What Would Happen Without Nuclear Power?

Japan was a good example of what a country looks like after shutting down its reactors. After the Fukushima disaster, Japan decided to halt the operation of nuclear power plants indefinitely. The electricity prices in Japan rose over 20 percent and pollution worsened. Nuclear power advocates believed the government should help the nuclear power industry. They said that nuclear power keeps costs low and is important for reducing greenhouse gases.

New safety standards have been developed in light of the disaster. Power plants believe they meet the new guidelines. Yet in an important court case, a judge said that safety is not guaranteed because another earthquake is always a possibility. Legal battles made restarting reactors a long and uncertain process.

Many people gather to protest the use of nuclear power plants in Japan on the anniversary of the Fukushima disaster.

People coming together to protest has a big effect. Nuclear power plants haven't been built because concerned citizens mobilized.

Some advocates for nuclear power feel that the biggest obstacle to new nuclear technology is public protests. They believe that most people don't understand the advantages of nuclear power. Advocates say that the public should give nuclear reactors a chance.

Much of our worry about nuclear power comes from issues of trust. We rely on experts to tell us if we are protected against radiation we can't see. We count on the government to evaluate risks and make laws to protect us. We hope businesses will make smart decisions and run nuclear power plants responsibly. But people are behind all of these decisions. People make mistakes. People also disagree. One scientist says low doses of radiation are safe. Another says low levels of radiation are very dangerous. It's hard to know whom to trust. In the end, time will give us more information about long-term effects of nuclear technology. Disasters teach us how to do things differently.

What we know for certain is that we face an energy crisis. As fossil fuels run out, our energy use continues to increase. We need to find a solution. To do so requires making difficult decisions. Every generation must decide: Is nuclear power worth the risks?

CRITICAL THINKING

- Do you think that nuclear fusion is a better process than nuclear fission? Why?

- Why do you think President Carter decided to stop nuclear power plants from reprocessing plutonium?

- How would life be different without nuclear power?

- Why is high-level nuclear waste dangerous?

- Why is it better to live in an energy independent country than a country that is energy dependent?

- Do you think that America will continue to use nuclear power? Why or why not?

- Are you for or against nuclear power? Why?

Glossary

Acute Radiation Syndrome (ARS) An illness that occurs following exposure to high levels of radiation.

atom The smallest unit of ordinary matter.

chain reaction A continuous process in which the nucleus of an atom is split, releasing neutrons that split other nuclei.

clean energy An energy source that does not release pollutants.

climate change The increase in the planet's temperature which will lead to droughts, flooding, and other extreme weather.

fossil fuels Coal, oil, and natural gas.

greenhouse gases The pollution produced by fossil fuels.

isotopes Different forms of the same element.

liquidators The name for the six hundred thousand people who cleaned up radioactive debris following the Chernobyl disaster.

neutron The part of an atom's nucleus that is not positively nor negatively charged.

nuclear fission Splitting the nucleus of an atom to produce energy.

nuclear fusion Bringing together the nuclei of two different atoms to produce energy.

nuclear reactor The part of the nuclear power plant where chain reactions occur.

nuclear waste The by-products of nuclear power plants. Usually refers to spent fuel rods.

radiation The energy a particle gives off when it decays.

regulation A rule or law.

reprocess To transform a by-product of nuclear fission, such as plutonium, into usable fuel for nuclear reactors.

spent rod A uranium fuel rod that has been used up.

subsidy Money given by the government to offset costs.

Find Out More

Books

Bailey, Diane. *Harnessing Energy: Nuclear Power*. Harnessing Energy Series. Mankato, MN: The Creative Company, 2015.

Lusted, Greg. *A Nuclear Power Plant*. Building History Series. San Diego, CA: KidHaven Press, 2005.

Rissman, Rebecca. *The Chernobyl Disaster*. History's Greatest Disasters. Minneapolis, MN: Core Library, 2013.

Websites

The Environmental Protection Agency

www.epa.gov/radiation/understand/calculate.html

The EPA site features an interactive radiation calculator that tallies your dose of radiation in a year.

How Nuclear Power Works

science.howstuffworks.com/nuclear-power.htm

This in-depth series covers the process or nuclear fission, the pros and cons of nuclear power, and the design of nuclear power plants. The website provides animations, diagrams, and easy-to-follow explanations. Environmental and economic topics are also covered.

National Geographic Education

education.nationalgeographic.com/education/encyclopedia/nuclear-energy

National Geographic's nuclear energy encyclopedia entry has an extensive glossary and slide show.

Understanding Science: Cold Fusion

www.undsci.berkeley.edu/article/0_0_0/cold_fusion_01

The Understanding Science team looks at the history of cold fusion and explains how Martin Fleischmann and Stanley Pons failed to meet scientific standards.

Index

Page numbers in **boldface** are illustrations. Entries in **boldface** are glossary terms.

About the Author

Caitlyn Paley lives in Maryland, where she works in classrooms and writes books for young readers. She has written several books for Cavendish Square Press, including *Slave Narratives and the Writings of Freedmen* and *Strategic Inventions of the Revolutionary War*. Paley enjoys doing research, hiking, trying new desserts, and exploring the world.